D1744585

About this Book

How many of us know about the religion of others? Why do some of our friends, and people that we see every day, have different beliefs from our own?

Jews and Judaism outlines the history of the Jewish people from Abraham to the present day, showing their religious development and the very close links between their belief that God chose their nation for his special favour, and their interpretation of their own varied and often disastrous history.

Their religion has always tended to emphasize the difference between themselves and all other people, and in spite of their dispersal throughout many countries of the world, the Jewish religion and way of life has been preserved.

In the following pages Leonard Hobley tells the fascinating story of the Jews and their religion.

Beliefs and Believers

by Leonard F. Hobley

JEWS AND JUDAISM
CHRISTIANS AND CHRISTIANITY
MOSLEMS AND ISLAM

BUDDHISTS AND BUDDHISM   Martha Patrick
HINDUS AND HINDUISM   Partha and Swasti Mitter
SIKHS AND SIKHISM   S. S. Kapoor

JEWS AND JUDAISM

Leonard F. Hobley

First published in 1979 by
Wayland (Publishers) Ltd
49 Lansdowne Place, Hove
East Sussex, BN3 1HF, England

Copyright © 1979 by Wayland (Publishers) Ltd

Second impression 1982

4th impression 1984

ISBN 0 85340 712 6

Printed and bound in Great Britain

Contents

1 Who are the Jews?

What makes a person a Jew? Does he have to believe in the religion of Judaism, or does belief in Judaism make him a Jew? Do all Jews speak a Jewish language? Can you recognize them by their appearance?

Who then are they? In early times it was fairly clear who were the Jews, or Israelites as they were then called. They were a tribe with their own language and customs, out of which grew their own religion and idea of God.

They were a branch of the Semitic people, which included Egyptians, Syrians, Phoenicians and Babylonians. All had similar features and spoke languages which were much alike. If the Israelites had continued to live in the land of Canaan (Palestine), modern Jews would probably have looked similar to other Semitic peoples. Some of them still do, but for nineteen hundred years the Jews have been scattered over much of the world, and have mixed with other nations, and people of other races have adopted the Jewish religion.

It seems then that there is nothing particular about a Jew's appearance. As to language, in everyday life most Jews speak the language of the country in which they live, although some Jews still use Yiddish for conversation amongst themselves. This language has been widely used among some European Jews since the Middle Ages, based upon medieval German with some Hebrew and Slavic. Religious Jews use the ancient Hebrew language for study and prayer. So there is no one language spoken in everyday life by all Jews.

The beliefs of religious Jews lead them to wear special clothes, such as little skull caps in home and synagogue. Many Jews eat only certain foods, but today not all of them keep these religious customs, so in this too it is not easy to recognize a Jew.

Many Jews brought up in the Jewish religious way of life, later give it up. Some even become atheists, believing in no god and no religion. Are they no longer Jews? And do non-Jews become Jews if they adopt Judaism? Is a person a Jew because of race, religion, family, or what? We hope in the following pages to supply the answers to these questions.

A young Jewish boy in Israel

2 The Origins of Judaism

Judaism has a longer ancestry than most religions, and is still a living religion today, practised by Jews in almost every country in the world. It is also the parent religion from which Christianity and Islam developed.

Like most religions, Judaism probably arose from worship of nature gods in early times. Modern ideas about religion are very different from when Judaism and other faiths were developing. In the early stages of most religions, people had no idea of the laws of nature which control the universe. They thought the sun, moon and stars were created especially to give light and warmth to the earth and that, if he wished, God could make the sun stand still!

Early religious thinkers tried to explain the wonders and disasters around them by telling stories, and for centuries these stories and legends were believed to be true and it was considered wicked to question them. Gradually men realized that they were not scientifically true, but the mass of people still clung to the old beliefs.

In early parts of the Old Testament God is sometimes shown as jealous and bloodthirsty, but later the Jewish Bible speaks of him as kind and loving. Judaism is therefore an interesting example of how Man's ideas of religion and God have changed.

Judaism began nearly four thousand years ago, when a man named Abraham decided to move, with his flocks and herds, away from his homeland in Mesopotamia. He believed that God wished to make a covenant (bargain) with him, that in return for obedience and worship he and his descendants should live in the land of Canaan, and that they would become a great nation. This is why Jews are sometimes called 'The Chosen People'. Abraham's descendants became the twelve tribes of Israel, the Israelites.

Abraham believed that this god was the true God and he called him Yahweh. Most people at that time worshipped many gods, but Abraham came to believe that this one god was especially interested in him and his family, and that they should worship only him. Gradually, as the centuries passed, the Israelites came to think of Yahweh as the only God, creator of the universe; and they looked back to Abraham as the founder of their nation and their religion.

They thought of him as the ideal man, upright, devout and completely obedient to God. So obedient that according to the story, when he

Abraham and his family journeying to Canaan with their flocks

thought God wanted him to sacrifice his beloved son Isaac, he bound him on an altar and was about to plunge in the knife, when he heard God telling him not to harm the boy. This story tells us that the Israelites' idea of God had changed – they no longer thought that God required human sacrifice, although other tribes in the region were still doing so.

Abraham and his tribe settled in Canaan and his idea of Yahweh, the special God of his people, was not forgotten. Many years later famine forced the Israelites to leave Canaan and go to Egypt. When they reached Egypt they were captured and made slaves.

An Egyptian wall painting depicting the Israelites arriving in Egypt

3 Moses and the Exodus

After many years of slavery, Moses, one of the greatest teachers and lawgivers, led the Israelite slaves out of Egypt, through the desert of Sinai, and united them into a nation.

Like Abraham, he had heard the voice of God, telling him to rescue his people from their slavery in Egypt. He warned Pharaoh (the king) that Yahweh, God of the Israelites, would bring disasters upon the Egyptians unless the Israelites were allowed to go free.

Terrible plagues came to Egypt but Pharaoh would not agree to let them go until Moses threatened that the Lord Yahweh would kill the first born in every house in Egypt, except those of the Israelites. The Book of Exodus says: "There was a great cry in Egypt, for there was not a house where there was not one dead." But, according to the story, the angel of death passed over the houses of the Israelites because they painted their doorposts with a special sign.

At last Pharaoh agreed to free the Israelites, and they left Egypt. This Exodus, the escape from slavery, has been celebrated ever since in the feast of the Passover.

Next Moses said that God had commanded him to go up Mount Sinai to receive instructions for the people. Moses climbed the mountain, where he heard God speaking to him. Then he came down and told them that God had given him a set of rules by which they must live. "God has made a covenant (bargain) with you, that he will lead you to the promised Land of Canaan, and bless and protect all future generations of the Israelites, for you are his Chosen People. In return, you must obey his commandments."

Moses, by the Italian sculptor Michelangelo

4 Commandments and Laws

The most important rules are known as the Ten Commandments. The first four state the Israelites' duty to God: they must not worship other gods or make carved images of them, must not take the name of God in vain, and must keep the Sabbath day holy in God's honour. The fifth commands the honouring of parents, and the rest forbid murder, theft, adultery, false witness (lying) and covetousness (envy).

Moses also gave the people instructions on peace offerings and animal sacrifices: how they should be killed, and how the blood should be sprinkled, and the meat burned on the altar, as "a sweet savour unto the Lord". Other instructions covered every aspect of their lives: marriage and family affairs, release of slaves, cancelling of debts, and rules of health and cleanliness which included what they were allowed to eat and drink, and how the foods were to be prepared. The poor were to be helped; at harvest time the corners of the fields were not to be reaped, but left for the poor to gather. They must not hate their brothers; they must love their neighbours as themselves.

As these laws were regarded as God's commands, they formed part of their religion. This belief that Yahweh was their own God, interested in their doings, and promising them a great future, did much to bind the Israelites into a nation, and encouraged them in times of danger.

Moses realized that commandments alone would not keep the Israelites to their correct behaviour and worship of Yahweh. When they felt things were not going well, they grumbled and were easily persuaded that Yahweh was not interested in them. Moses therefore gave them a symbol around which their religious ceremonies could be centred. This was a tent called the Tabernacle, which could be set up wherever the Israelites camped on their way to the Promised Land. Inside the Tabernacle was the Ark of the Covenant, containing the stone tablets with the Ten Commandments inscribed on them.

Moses shows his brother Aaron the Ten Commandments

Although he had made a nation out of a slave people, and had given them a complete religion and code of conduct, Moses did not live to lead them into the Promised Land. After forty years of wandering between Egypt and Canaan, he died in about 1100 B.C. Joshua, his successor, called the people together and after many battles, led them back into Canaan, which was shared out among the twelve tribes.

Joshua leading the Israelites triumphantly back into Canaan

Setting up the Tabernacle in the wilderness

5 Kings and Prophets

For a long time the Israelites were ruled by judges. During this period they were often attacked and overcome by neighbouring peoples, and then the ruling judge would preach that Yahweh was angry with them for worshipping strange gods and had given them into the hands of their enemies as punishment. Samuel was the last judge. The Israelites asked for a king to rule them so Samuel chose a man named Saul to be their king.

The greatest king was David, Saul's successor. In the days of troubles that came later, the Israelites remembered David as the ideal king, successful in war against Israel's enemies, and favoured by Yahweh for his loyalty to Israel's religion. David captured Jerusalem and took the Ark of the Covenant there, making the city the centre of worship. When he was approaching death he said to his son Solomon, "I go the way of all the earth; be thou strong, therefore, and show thyself a man."

Solomon believed in doing things in style: he wished to show to the world his power and wealth as king of the Israelites. He built a temple of stone and cedar-wood for the worship of Yahweh in Jerusalem in which the Ark of the Covenant was placed, and this remained the centre of worship until the temple was

King David playing the harp

destroyed many years later. He also built a palace four times larger than the temple where he lived in great luxury with seven hundred wives.

The rule of Solomon and his son led to discontent, and about 930 B.C.

The prophet Elijah was believed to have ascended into heaven in a chariot of fire

the kingdom of the Israelites broke up, and formed the two kingdoms of Judah and Israel.

The Israelites continued to lose faith in Yahweh and sometimes went back to their old ways of worshipping false gods. When this happened their teachers, who they called prophets, would preach to them and warn of Yahweh's anger if they neglected his commandments and covenants made with Abraham and Moses.

The greatest prophets were Elijah and Isaiah. They continually warned the Israelites to mend their ways and told them that Yahweh did not want bloodshed but for them to show kindness and justice to others. Isaiah looked forward to the time

when all would recognize the God of the Israelites as "the Lord of all the earth". He said, "And he (God) shall judge among the nations, and shall rebuke many peoples, and they shall beat their swords into ploughshares and their spears into pruning hooks; nation shall not lift up sword against nation, neither shall they learn war any more."

above
King Solomon dictating his proverbs.
He was known to be very wise

16

6 The Captivity

The hopes of the prophets were shattered, for in 722 B.C. the Assyrians destroyed the kingdom of Israel and carried off its people to captivity from which they never returned. For a time Judah managed to retain a precarious independence, but finally in 587 B.C. it too fell, and many of the people were carried off to Babylon.

Cut off from their God-given homeland and their temple, the Israelites, or Jews as they were beginning to be called, turned more and more to their religious scriptures, and the traditions of their God's promise to bring them peace and happiness. Yet they could not understand why they had to suffer so much and undergo such hardship and exile. They tried to explain it as punishment for sin, not just of individuals, but of the Jewish nation. But some felt that the mystery of suffering was insoluble and that God's ways must be accepted.

While they were in exile the Jews were influenced by other religions, particularly that of Zoroaster, who believed there was one God who would bring about the triumph of good over evil. Theirs was a religion of hope, and it appealed to

Assyrian soldiers lead the defeated Israelites into captivity

17

the Jews, who in spite of exile, slavery and persecution, never gave up hope that in time God would rescue them from their unhappiness in captivity and return them to their Promised Land'.

The King of Babylon, watching while Israelite captives are killed

7 Changing Ideas of God and Hopes of a Messiah

Most of the books of the Old Testament were written during the Captivity and after. The book of Genesis gives what might be called a modern view of the creation of the world, for it proclaimed that the universe was the creation of one force, a natural order, not a jumble of animal gods, sun gods and man-like gods. It also said that the whole created world was good.

The following books show how the writers were groping after a fuller understanding of Man, and a developing idea of God. Most Israelites thought of God, not as a local deity, but as the creator of the universe and as just, merciful and loving. But, could such a God of the universe choose one small nation, and favour it above all others? And would he lead them in war to conquer the land of other peoples? How could such a belief be a satisfactory guide to religion and life?

From a narrow and self-centred idea of God, some Jews began to work out a religion which they believed could unite all races. It was

An old Jewish print showing how they imagined Elijah would lead the Messiah to Jerusalem

ירושלם

very difficult for them to accept such ideas as they had always believed themselves to be 'God's Chosen people', and most Jews kept their ancient beliefs.

Their suffering in captivity continued, and they came under the rule of several different nations. Many Jews had become lazy about religion, but others called the Hasidim (Righteous) called for a return to the old true faith and, led by the Maccabees, they rebelled against their ruler. They suffered torture and death rather than betray their religion, and their martyrdom encouraged others to resist and so saved Judaism from dying out.

During these tragic experiences the belief grew that God would send them a Messiah (leader) to deliver them from their sufferings. Jesus, the Jewish founder of Christianity, was proclaimed as this Messiah and he taught that distinctions between nations would be swept away, and all peoples would live together in love.

Most Jews could not accept that there was no special relationship between them and God, and when Jesus taught that there are no chosen people, no favourites in God's eyes, their intense patriotism and religious traditions combined to make them angrily reject his teachings. So although Christianity arose out of Judaism, it failed to convince the Jews. In fact, there was great enmity between Jews and Christians. The Jews thought it blasphemy for Christians to claim Jesus as the divine son of God, while the Christians hated the Jews for

encouraging their Roman rulers to crucify him. This caused bitter hatred between Jews and Christians and has led to persecution and abuse of Jews for centuries.

Jesus, the Jewish founder of Christianity

8 The Diaspora

In A.D. 70 the Romans destroyed Jerusalem and drove many Jews from Canaan, then named Palestine. It was to be nearly 2000 years before they returned to their 'Promised Land'. At first they fled mainly to cities in neighbouring countries where they usually found groups of different races, each occupying separate districts, speaking their own language and worshipping their own gods. There were already Jewish communities in some of these cities, and these were enlarged or new ones formed. Through the Bible and their religious education, they remained as conscious as ever of their Jewish unity, and their differences from their neighbours. Everywhere they refused to worship any gods but their own true God.

Some went to Egypt where there was a large Jewish community in Alexandria, following many different trades. Jewish merchants prospered, and many settled in Italian cities. Others went to Spain,

Where the Jews went to when they left Palestine, up to the end of the nineteenth century. The numbers on the map refer to the centuries in which Jews settled in that part of the world

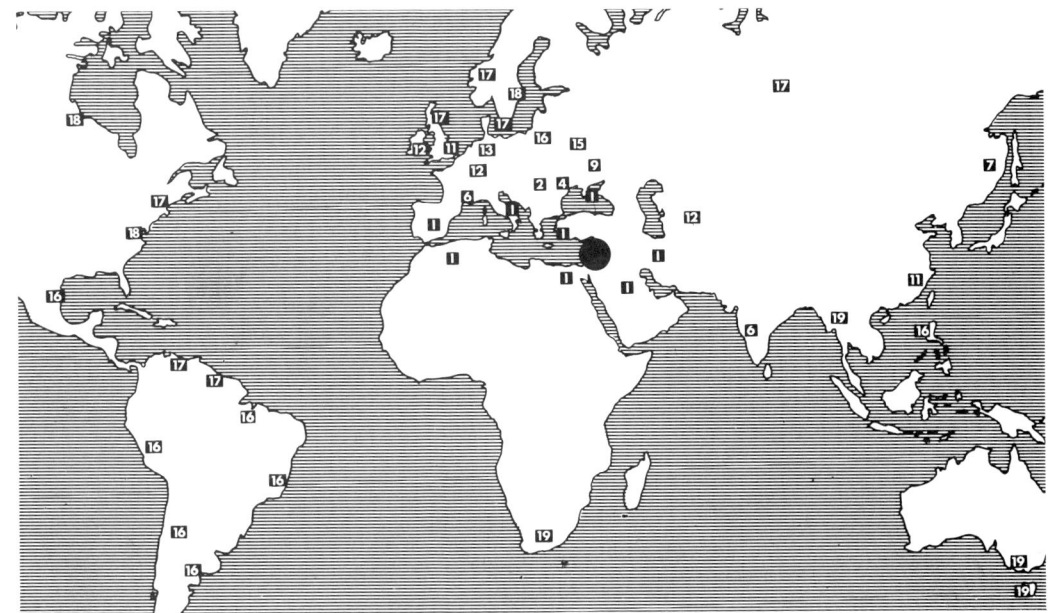

France, Britain, Germany, Poland and Russia, and some passed outside the Roman Empire in the east to Babylonia and Assyria. Jews who settled in northern and eastern Europe were called Ashkenazim, and those who settled in countries around the Mediterranean were called Sefardim.

The first Christians were Jews, but Paul, the great Christian missionary and himself a Jew, turned to the gentiles for converts. Most Jews of the Diaspora kept to their own faith, and increasingly ill feeling grew

Roman relief showing the looting and destruction of the Temple in Jerusalem

between Jews and Christians, particularly when rulers made Christianity the official religion of their countries. Jews were then often persecuted.

When Mohammed proclaimed the Moslem faith in the seventh century A.D., and himself as the last and greatest prophet of the God whom the Jews worshipped, he expected the Jews would convert easily to the new religion. When they refused, there was some persecution and killing of Jews, but later the Moslem Arabs and the Jews lived for centuries in friendship, each tolerating the other's religion. But when the Christians reconquered Spain, every Jew who refused to become a Christian was driven out. Jews were frequently persecuted in most Christian countries.

Moslems proclaiming the message of Mohammed and spreading the faith of Islam

9 Persecution

Feelings against Jews grew firstly because they were amongst those who urged the Romans to kill Christ. Thereafter, increasing persecution encouraged them to shun the company of non-Jews, and they gained a reputation of believing themselves to be superior. As Christian laws prevented them from owning land, and Christian guilds prohibited them from learning crafts, the Jews were forced to stay in the cities, and to follow urban rather than agricultural trades. Their occupations were often restricted, therefore, to money lending and trading. Jews also often became financiers, and built up an international network of bankers. Kings found them useful and used them to raise loans and collect taxes. This made them unpopular with traders and the public, and perhaps for this reason Jews have a reputation, amongst non-Jews, for avarice.

In many cities the Jews were forced by law to live in walled districts called ghettos, where they were locked in at night. They were deprived of ordinary civil rights, and had to wear yellow Star of David badges.

Organized persecution began with the First Crusade. In France and Germany crusaders dragged Jewish families into the street, forcibly baptizing them, and if they refused to give up their religion they were murdered. Some Jews strangled their children and then killed themselves, rather than submit to enforced Christianity.

After that, in times of disaster, the Jews were often made the scapegoats. When the Black Death struck Europe in 1349 there were pogroms (massacres) of Jews in many places, when bands of Christians killed whole Jewish communities, claiming that the Jews were spreading the plague in order to wipe out the Christians. Since the Jews kept their ghettos cleaner than the Christian parts of cities, fewer Jews died of the plague, and they were then accused of witchcraft.

Gradually the treatment of Jews improved. In England, in the seventeenth century, Oliver Cromwell allowed Jews, banished since 1290, to resettle, and worship as they wished. Nowadays, prayers are said

A medieval satire on the Jews showing them as evil money-lenders

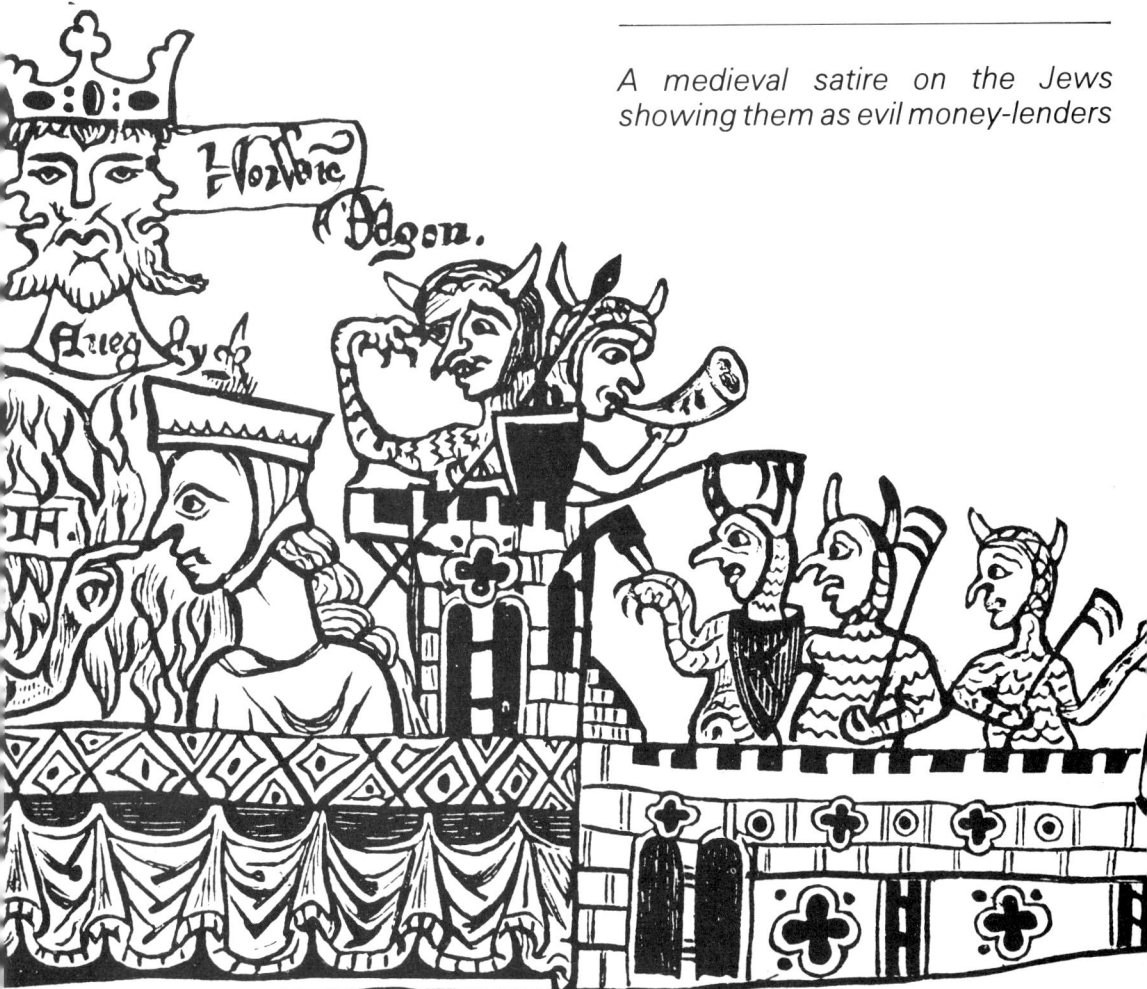

in the synagogues for the Queen, the Royal Family and the British government.

In Russia, however, Jews continued to be very badly treated. In 1881 a terrible series of pogroms began, and thousands of Jewish refugees fled to America, Britain, and parts of western Europe, where their arrival caused an increase in anti-Jewish feeling.

left

The expulsion of the Jews from Czarist Russia in the nineteenth century

The torturing of Jews by Christians, who accused them of being heretics and witches

10 Religion, the Rabbi and the Synagogue

The Jews base their religion upon their scriptures: the Pentateuch (the first five books of the Bible), contains the covenants made by Abraham and Moses with God, the laws and practices laid down by Moses, and the books written by the prophets.

The Torah lists these laws, and the fundamental human rights. It also states a Jew's duties: to show concern for the poor and those in distress. The main laws and teachings, together with history and stories, were brought together in the Talmud in the fourth and fifth centuries A.D.

Right
Prayer book with Jewish prayer shawls

Inside an Orthodox synagogue

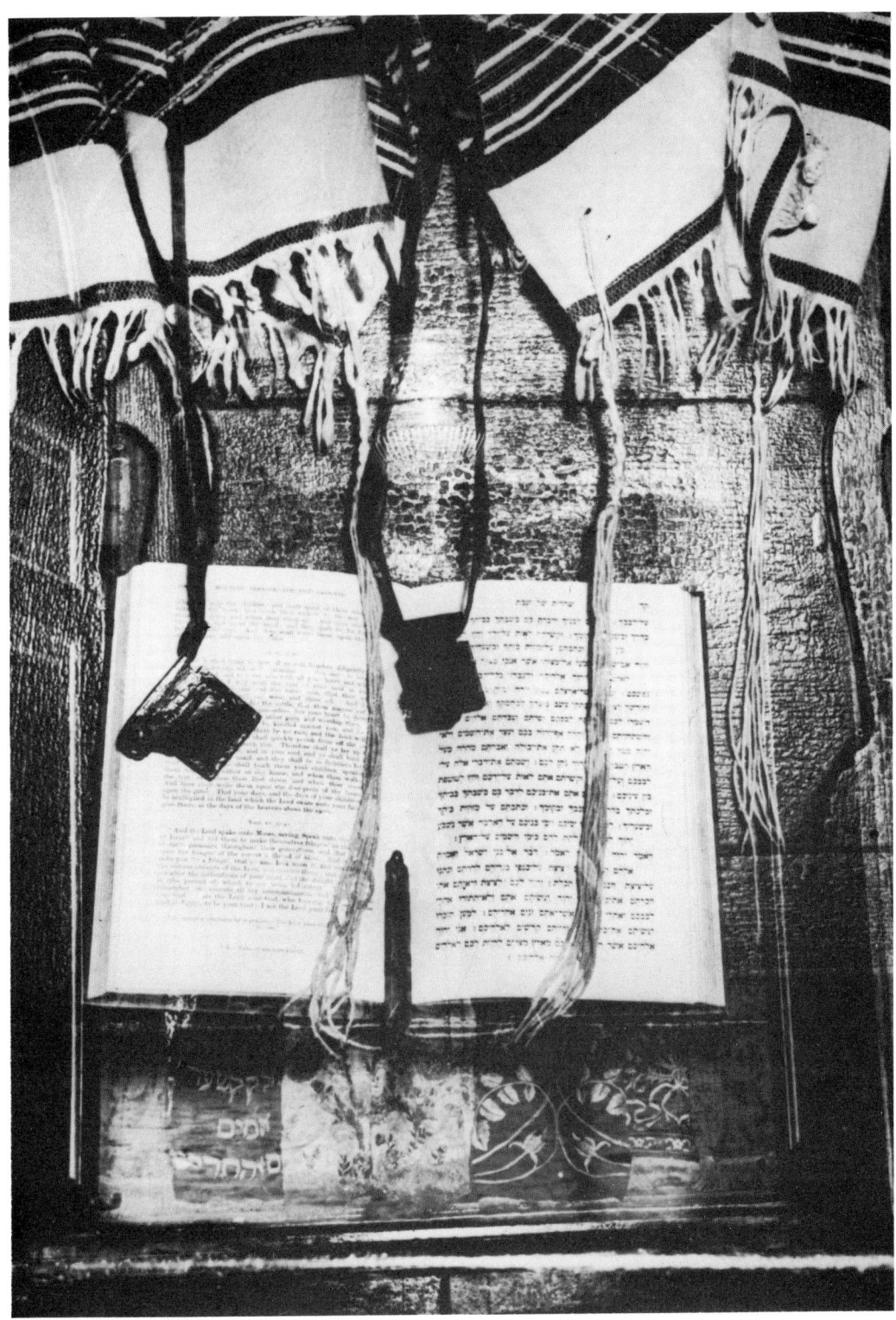

Hebrew scholars studied the Law and the Scriptures, producing commentaries, and sometimes different interpretations. Over 2000 years ago these scholars were given the title of Rabbi which means Master, and Jewish communities have ever since looked to them for guidance on points of law and way of life. Rabbis have always aimed at the preservation of Hebrew wisdom, and have done all they could to ensure that their distinctive way of life was not weakened in any way.

It was their duty to search the scriptures for new and better guidance for belief and behaviour. Since, to the Jews, all behaviour is guided by God's laws, the rabbis had to study not only the religious writings, but also botany, physiology, mathematics, and astronomy, so that they could decide the correct timing of ceremonies, the correct interpretation of the laws of diet, and so on. The rabbi today continues to act as leader, teacher and preacher.

When Jerusalem was captured by the Babylonians in 587 B.C., Solomon's temple was burned down, and the Ark of the Covenant was destroyed. Jews then carried out their worship in various places, and new forms of service were introduced. During the fourth and third centuries B.C. these services took place in synagogues, which have become the regular place for worship ever since. The synagogue is much more than a place of worship, it is the centre for all types of communal and social activities, as well as for study and religious training.

At congregational worship, one of the scrolls of the Torah is brought out from the Ark, basically a cupboard on the wall of the synagogue which faces Jerusalem. It is carried in procession round the synagogue, and members of the congregation bow towards it. A lamp burns, as a reminder of the seven-branched candalabrum which burned continually in the temple in Jerusalem. Men keep their heads covered in the synagogue, and sit separately from women. There are three set times for prayers; morning, afternoon and evening. Every Jew learns` the Shema; 'Hear O Israel, the Lord is our God, the Lord is One': the first prayer learnt by children and the last prayer of the dying.

The Menorah

30

12   The Jewish Home

A Jewish house is regarded as a shrine as well as a home. At the entrance is a mezuzah, a small receptacle containing the Shema. Jews often lay an extra place at table on the Sabbath and at Passover, ready for a possible guest, remembering the hospitality shown by Abraham, the founder of the Israelite people, whose tent was always open to guests.

It is the Jewish wife's duty to see that the children understand and carry out the religious observances. An important part of her life is to see that meals are prepared according to the dietary laws, which say what foods must and must not be eaten, and how they must be prepared and cooked.

The dietary laws contained in the Torah are very comprehensive. Jews must not eat the flesh of winged insects, of creeping things, or of animals except those which chew the cud and have cloven hoofs. They must not eat fish except those with scales and fins, or birds of prey and carrion eaters.

A Jewish family at home in Israel celebrating Seder, the Feast of the Passover

34

Blood must not be consumed, for according to the Bible blood is life, and life must be returned to God. Animals which are eaten must be killed in such a way that the blood drains out of the body. This is done by slitting the throat in a certain way with a very sharp knife. The meat must be soaked in water and then in salt, and finally rinsed thoroughly. Food properly prepared and cooked is called kosher, that is, acceptable according to Jewish law.

You may ask, Why mustn't a Jew eat pork? Or oysters, or shrimps? Why mustn't a Jew eat yorkshire pudding with his roast beef if the pudding is made with milk? What have these things to do with religion?

The strict Jew will answer that these are God's commandments and must not be questioned. The Bible says, "Thou shalt not seethe (boil) a kid in its mother's milk", and this has been developed into a law which says meat may not be eaten in the same meal as anything containing milk. Strict Jews will not eat any dairy food until several hours have passed since eating meat. Separate sets of dishes, pans and cloths are kept for meat and dairy dishes.

Some of the dietary rules may have originally been made for health reasons, and Jews are reminded at every meal, of God's goodness in providing the food. Each meal begins and ends with a blessing. The Jews have always emphasized their differences from other people, and their strict diet is a constant reminder. They attach great importance to not eating pork as the Torah forbids them to eat pigs. This was so important to them that at the time of the Maccabees, when they were offered the choice of eating pork or being tortured and killed, they chose death. Many Jews would not think it so important nowadays, and they differ in their attitudes to dietary rules.

A Jewish shop in England selling only kosher meat and poultry

13   The Sabbath

Most Jewish festivals date from early times, and commemorate important events in the history of the Israelites. The keeping of the Sabbath refers to even earlier events, for it is held in honour of God, the creator of the universe, as told in the book of Genesis, when he rested on the seventh day, after the work of creation. Genesis tells that God saw that what he had created was good, so the Sabbath is a day of thankfulness for the goodness of life, and the beauty and wonder of creation. Keeping the Sabbath is also connected with Jewish history, for the day of rest and happiness is such a contrast to the slavery of the Israelites in Egypt.

The Sabbath is observed from sunset on Friday to nightfall on Saturday, and during that time, no work is done, for the word Sabbath means rest. It is a family day celebrated in the home. When the parents return from the Friday evening service at the synagogue, they pronounce a blessing on the children. The mother then lights the Sabbath candles, and the father gives thanks for his wife, "whose price is far above rubies", and the home.

The family then sits down to a special meal. The table is spread with the best linen, and two loaves are placed on it as a reminder of the

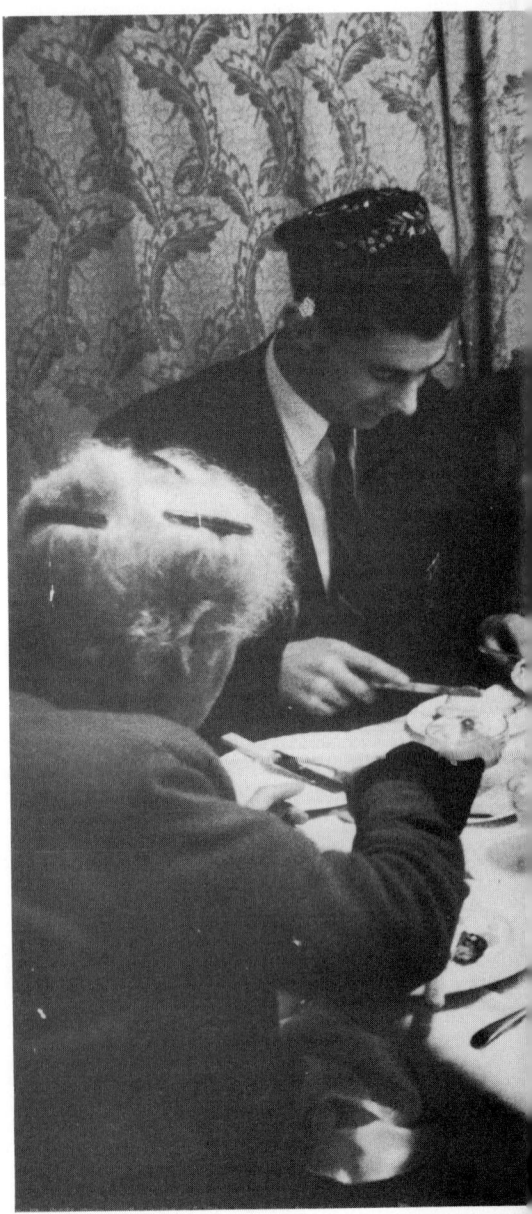

double portion of manna (food) which God gave the Israelites when they were wandering in the wilderness. Wine is blessed and shared, the loaves are broken, and the meal begins.

The Sabbath morning service recalls how Moses brought down the commandments from the Mount, including the importance of observing the Sabbath. The day ends with the dousing of the candles.

A Jewish family eats by candlelight on the Sabbath eve

14   Customs and Festivals

Passover is an eight-day festival to celebrate the Exodus of the Israelites from Egypt. At the beginning of Passover. Seder (the Passover feast) is celebrated in the home and the youngest member asks, "Why is this night different from all other nights?" The father

The Scroll of the Law carried through the streets of Manchester

The blowing of the Shofar heralds the Jewish New Year

replies, "Because we were slaves under Pharaoh in Egypt and God brought us forth out of Egypt." Unleavened bread and bitter herbs are eaten, to remind them of the hardships of slavery, and of their hurried flight. They also drink wine and sing psalms, rejoicing in the freedom which God gave them.

The Jewish New Year is celebrated in autumn with ten days of penitence, culminating in Yom Kippur, the Day of Atonement. This is the holiest day of the year, when no food or drink is taken, sins are confessed, and Jews are reconciled with God. A blast on the Shofar (ram's horn) in the synagogue, heralds Jewish New Year's Day and calls the Jews to repentance.

There are many other festivals celebrating events in Jewish history, and customs which emphasize the difference between Jews and other peoples. One way of emphasizing their difference is the custom of circumcision.

From their earliest boyhood Jews are taught that they are different from others, and are God's 'Chosen People'. All Jewish boys are circumcised eight days after birth, as stipulated in the covenant God made with Abraham, according to Genesis. This is an operation in which the loose skin is cut from the male sexual organ. It is a permanent reminder of the Jews' long religious history, of how the decendants of Abraham proudly distinguished themselves from the surrounding tribes by being circumcised. Circumcision has been practised in many parts of the world, including ancient Egypt, from which the Israelites may have learned it; There may have been medical and health reasons, or it may have grown from the idea of sacrifice to a god of fertility. It is widely practised today by many people who are not Jews.

Left
Jews of the Middle Ages, at Passover

Jewish wedding in an Orthodox synagogue

15 Anti-semitism

In the eighteenth and nineteenth centuries anti-semitism (hostility to Jews) died down, and in the USA, and countries of western Europe, Jews gradually gained full rights of citizenship. They could own land, attend university, vote, and become members of parliament; and they could worship as they wished. In our own twentieth century, however, anti-semitism again became common, especially in Europe.

After the First World War, most east European countries signed agreements to guarantee civic and religious rights to minorities, including Jews. But soon intense national feeling in Poland led to increasing anti-Jewish activity. This was partly due to a revival of the old anti-Jewish feeling, and partly to envy at Jewish success in commerce.

The Russian revolution in 1917 brought many changes for the Jews. One of the first acts of the Provisional Government was to abolish all restrictions on Jews, but a few months later the Bolshevik revolution brought less welcome changes.

A burning synagogue in Europe during the 1930s

Jews wearing the Star of David are forced to leave their homes

Victimization of Jews in Poland

It ended the anti-semitic influence of the Orthodox (Russian) Church, but allowed Jews rights only if they lived in specific territories, and they were spread throughout Russia.

During the civil war which followed the revolution, those fighting against the Communists saw the Jews as enemies, and killed thousands of them in wide-spread pogroms. After the civil war the government tried to force the Jews to adopt communist ideas, and Jewish schools and communities were taken over. As with all other religions, Judaism was frowned upon, and religious instruction of Jewish children was forbidden.

The Jews were becoming more unpopular. People in Moscow were asking; Why did the Jews keep to themselves and hold their own beliefs and customs, instead of mixing with others like good Soviet citizens? In 1929 the Five Year Plan called for greatly increased industrial development, and trade schools were opened, training Jews for industry. Many political leaders friendly to the Jews were assassinated during the 1930s, and anti-semitism grew once more.

Persecution in Germany

Meanwhile even more terrible persecution was threatening elsewhere. The Nazis under Adolf Hitler had come to power in Germany. German Jews had felt themselves to be part of the fine German civilization and many Jews had fought and died in the German armies during the First World War. But Hitler had a terrible hatred of the Jews, whom he blamed for all Germany's misfortunes, and throughout the country they were humiliated and persecuted. When the Second World War began, Hitler took steps to exterminate the Jews altogether.

In Germany itself and all the countries which were overrun by the Germans, Jews were herded into concentration camps, where forced labour and starvation killed many of them.

About two million Jews fled to Russia or Russian-occupied Poland. There they had to adapt to Soviet organization and large numbers were deported to central Asia.

When Hitler invaded Russia in June 1941, three-and-a-half million Jews were in great danger. Those who could, fled to the east, but nearly two million fell into Hitler's hands, and he began to have them exterminated in specially built gas chambers. By the end of the war six million Jews—men, women and children—had been murdered by the Nazis. It was no wonder that the survivors hoped more than ever to be able to return again to their 'Promised Land'.

These people are being taken away to a concentration camp

Persecution in the Soviet Union

After the war, there were about two million Jews in the Soviet Union who were refugees from Poland, Romania, and other parts of eastern Europe. Most of these were sent back to their own countries, where they were often unwelcome.

In the Soviet Union itself opinion was changing. In 1948 Stalin supported the setting up of the Jewish state of Israel in Palestine, but soon afterwards he changed his mind. He wanted all in Russia to consider themselves as Soviet citizens, and nothing else. It was denied that there could be a Jewish nation. The Jewish state was condemned as a tool of American and British capitalists. The old suspicions and hatred of Jews easily revived and the Jews were described as money-lenders and capitalists. Jewish writers were arrested, and some killed or deported. They were dismissed from service in the army, foreign affairs, and foreign trade.

Various accusations against the Jews were summed up in the charge of 'anti-Soviet activities'. Some Jews who wanted to leave the Soviet Union and go to Israel were refused permission, and sometimes brought to trial as dissidents, where they were publicly insulted, and sometimes sentenced to long periods in labour camps. For those who obtained permission to leave, emigration was made as difficult as possible. This attitude towards Jewish emigrants to Israel is still maintained in Russia today.

A Russian Jew's belongings are shared between Bolsheviks, during the Revolution

16   A Homeland at Last

Most Jews have always dreamed of a return to the Promised Land. But not until late in the nineteenth century did this appear to be more than a dream. In 1882 Baron de Rothschild, a French Jew, was struck by the wretched state of persecuted Jews in eastern Europe. He decided to help them set up farming communities in Palestine and bought land and farming equipment for them.

In 1895 Theodor Herzl, a Viennese Jew, wrote a book, *The Jewish State*, in which he suggested that, with support from other countries, an Israeli state could be set up, and all the world's Jews could move to it. Many Jews accepted Herzl's ideas with enthusiasm, and worked for the setting up of a Jewish state in Palestine. They were called Zionists. The British Government was also interested in Herzl's idea of a Jewish homeland. In 1903 Britain offered the Zionists land in Uganda where such a state could be formed, but that was not what they had in mind. They wanted to settle in Palestine, where their ancestors had lived for centuries.

In 1917 Mr Balfour, the British Foreign Secretary, issued his 'Declaration' that the British Government favoured the establishment of a Jewish national home in Palestine, and that it would do its best to bring this about. What was meant by a national home was not clearly defined. The Zionists greeted the declaration enthusiastically as a promise of a state to be completely under Jewish rule.

After the 1914-18 war and defeat of Turkey, Palestine, which had been part of the Turkish Empire since 1516, was administered by the British Government, and Jewish immigrants started to trickle in.

Jewish refugees in transit to Israel

Theodore Herzl, who wrote 'The Jewish State' in 1895

48

By 1924, fifty thousand Jews had arrived, most of them young pioneers, who started work immediately, building roads, draining swamps and preparing the land, much of it desert, for settlement.

The first kibbutz was founded in 1909, and a great number were established between the two world wars. At the end of the second war, the trickle of immigrants swelled to a flood, and many of the dispossessed Jews who had escaped Hitler's concentration camps came to the country. But the British government, still administering Palestine and trying to keep peace between Jews and Arabs (whose ancestors had lived in the land for centuries), took steps to prevent the mass immigration of Jews. This resulted in a war being fought by some of the Jewish immigrants, who had formed themselves into guerilla bands to oppose British rule.

Israeli children celebrating Harvest Festival on a kibbutz

17 Different Sects in Judaism

Almost all Jews have accepted some changes in Jewish law. The Torah allowed slavery and polygamy; now Jewish law does not. Once all debts had to be remitted after seven years; not so today. The sacrifice of animals is no longer carried out.

Nowadays opinions vary as to how much of the traditional Jewish law and ceremonial should be retained. Orthodox Jews carry out all their ceremonies and rituals; they wear the kippah (small head-covering) always; pray at the pre-scribed times; keep the Sabbath strictly, and have their children trained in special religious schools. Their women find fulfilment in organizing the home and bringing up their children on strictly religious lines.

Early in the nineteenth century some German Jews formed Reform Judaism, and it spread rapidly in the United States. Reform Jews and Liberal Jews believe in studying the scriptures to see how they should be applied to the modern world and they feel that the true destiny of the Jewish people is to work within the various nations in which they live, to create the unity of all mankind.

A movement in America is Conservative Judaism, which occupies a midway point of view, and there are also secular Jews who have ceased to believe in Judaism, but who feel a loyalty to Jews generally. Some enthusias-tically supported the new Zionist state of Israel.

A Jewish patriarch in Djerba, in the twentieth century

A Rabbi in the synagogue for the Buchara sect in Jerusalem

18   A Jew's Beliefs Today

Most of the world's Jews do not live in the State of Israel, but are citizens of many other countries, where some of them adopt the ideas of the people with whom they live.

In 1967 all Jerusalem passed into Israel's hands. Some Israelis see Jerusalem as the Holy City, sacred to millions of members of three great religions, but others see it primarily as the ancient Jewish capital, now again the centre of Jewish life and religion, under complete Jewish control.

Much of the old enmity between members of different religions is gone. In 1942 the Council of Christians and Jews was set up in Britain to promote mutual understanding and goodwill. The presidents are the Archbishops of Canterbury and Westminster, the Chief Rabbi, and the Moderators of the Church of Scotland.

Today a Jew might say that Judaism is the right religion for him because it teaches the belief in one universal God; that God has a purpose for mankind; and that he has made that purpose known through Abraham, Moses and the prophets. He has chosen the Jews, not to give them power and privilege, but to give them the duty of showing the world God's love and purpose for mankind.It is a religion of hope, because it believes that good will triumph over evil. Through its laws on food and behaviour, it helps to give a kind of holiness to everything believers do in their everyday lives and sanctifies the enjoyment of the good things of life. It promises life after death for all who try to live according to God's laws; to be honest, to love justice and to do their best to help the poor and needy everywhere in the world.

The Torah is carried around the synagogue at the Festival of Joy, in Djerba

Glossary

Bar-Mitzvah (plural, B'nei Mitzvah) The ceremony at which a Jewish boy undertakes responsibility for his own religious life and duties, at the age of thirteen.

Canaan 'The Promised Land' which the Jews believe was promised by God to Abraham and his descendants. Now known as Israel.

Diaspora The dispersal of the Jewish people throughout many countries when they were driven from Palestine by the Romans.

Gentile Anyone who is not a Jew.

Hebrew The ancient language of the Jews, and now the language of modern Israel.

Israeli Member of the modern state of Israel.

Israelites The ancient name for the Jews, descendants of Abraham, who became the twelve tribes of Israel.

Kibbutz A communal farming settlement in modern Israel. Everything is shared equally between all members. Women share equally with men in the work.

Kosher Food which in its origin and in its preparation is in accordance with Jewish laws.

Maccabees Followers of Maccabeus, an Israelite commander.

Menorah Seven or nine-branched candelabrum kept burning in the Temple at Jerusalem.

Messiah The saviour the Jews hoped God would send to deliver them from their captivity and bring about a world of peace.

Mezuzah A small receptacle which holds the Shema, the Jewish prayer.

Passover The festival commemorating the Israelites' escape from Egypt.

Patriarch The father and ruler of a family or a tribe.

Pentateuch The first five books of the Old Testament of the Bible.

Phylacteries Small leather containers with verses of scripture, worn by men at morning prayers.

Rabbi The chief official of a synagogue. A teacher and leader of students of the Torah.

Seder The Passover meal and ceremony in the home.

Semitic A race of people living in eastern Mediterannean countries.

Shema The first prayer learned by Jewish children, and last spoken by the dying.

Shofar The ram's horn blown as a signal to the people to repent on the Day of Atonement.

Synagogue The Jewish place of worship and meeting.

Tabernacle A tent in which the Israelites kept the Ark of the Covenant on their journey from Egypt to Canaan.

Talmud The sayings of Jewish rabbis about the laws of Moses, called the Mishnah, and the commentaries on them, called the Gemara.

Torah The revealed will of God as contained in the first five books of the Bible.

Yiddish A language used by Jews of the Diaspora, based upon medieval German, with some Hebrew and Slav words.

Yom Kippur The Day of Atonement, the last of the ten days of penitence at the Jewish New Year.

Zionism The movement for the return of the Jews to their 'Promised Land'.

More Books

A New Look at the Old Testament, Josephine Kamm. (Gollancz).

Gods and Men, B.W. Sherratt and D.J. Hawkin. (Blackie).

Judaism, Myer Domnitz. (Ward Lock Educational).

Religions of Mankind, H.K. Luke. (Christophers).

The History of World Religions, Katherine Savage. (Bodley Head).

The World's Living Religions, Geoffrey Parrender. (Pan Books).

Thinking about Judaism, Myer Domnitz. (Lutterworth).

World Faiths, Liva Baker. (Abelard-Schuman).

Index

Picture Acknowledgements

The author and publishers wish to thank all those who have given permission for copyright pictures to be reproduced on the following pages: Radio Times Hulton Picture Library, 7, 9, 10, 12, 13 upper and lower, 15, 20, 26-27, 28, 29, 31, 36-37, 38, 40, 41, 43, 44, 46-47, 52, 54, 57; Keystone Press Agency, 53; Pat Hodgson, 18, 23; Jewish Telegraph, 33 upper and lower, 39; Israel Information, 34, 49, 50-51, 55; Alfred Haagman, 32; The Trustees of the British Museum, 14. The remaining pictures are the property of the Wayland Picture Library.